MW01676290

1

Wisdom from India

ASTROLOGY

Wisdom from India 1

Vishal Mangalwadi

on

ASTROLOGY

from darkness to the Light
SOUTH ASIAN RESOURCES

Wisdom from India
ASTROLOGY

This SAR Booklet is published by

Nivedit Good Books Distributors Pvt. Ltd.
Ivy Cottage, Landour, Mussoorie (Uttaranchal),
India 248 179
Tel: + 91- (0) 135 63 0891
www.goodbookspubs.com

In North America order from:
South Asian Resources
Post Box 453, Willernie, MN 55090-0453
Tel: 651-426 4687
Fax: 651-426 4694
Email: SAResources@hotmail.com

Cover Design by C. Borsada

ISBN 81-86701-08-7

Printed in the United States of America

Acknowledgements

South Asian Resources is grateful to several people for their encouragement in launching this endeavour. SAR especially acknowledges the contribution of Professor Prabhu Guptara, Jenny Taylor and Ivan Kostka for the *Wisdom from India* series.

From the unreal lead me to the real
From darkness lead me to the light
From death lead me to immortality

Ancient Hindu prayer

Rig Veda

Contents

Preface

Hinduism is now a world religion. The Indian subcontinent exerts a global philosophical and cultural influence. Ideas and practices exported from South Asia have gained currency and even popularity in the West. Much of what is called "New Age" is rooted in the Hindu worldview.

Yet, most writings on subjects related to this trend, from Astrology to Yoga, tend to be either too scholarly or too simplistic, either by Western critics or Asian enthusiasts. South Asian Resources is bridging the gap with accessible yet responsible media resources that address ideas and issues of vital interest to both East and West. This series of booklets is just a beginning.

Vishal Mangalwadi is ideally suited to the task. An established Indian writer, he is passionate in his engagement with ideas of Indian origin and their practical impact on people's lives and wider culture. He is often described as a "different guru." He studied philosophy in secular Indian universities and Hindu ashrams as well as in L'Abri Fellowship, Switzerland. He has pioneered several creative projects for serving the poor in central India, and politically organized North India's "untouchables" and peasants.

This series of *Wisdom from India* booklets is for all who are interested in understanding and evaluating ideas and practices of South Asian origin. We trust it will stimulate your quest for satisfying answers.

Series Editor

ASTROLOGY IN THE RISE AND FALL OF ANCIENT CIVILIZATIONS

Does astrology really control our lives? If the tides of the ocean are substantially determined by the passage of the moon, if the moon influences the speed at which the earth rotates, then could it be that the moon's magnetic pull also affects the human body? After all, our bodies are at least 65 per cent water. Can we fully know ourselves without understanding the influence of the celestial bodies upon us? Astrology developed in ancient times as an attempt to understand the relationship between heavenly bodies and ourselves. It is interesting to study its consequences in cultures that believed in it seriously.

What made ancient China a great civilization? One minor factor was this: the Chinese sages understood that their rulers needed to be like the sun. They ought to exercise an authority in the human domain similar to that of the sun, which governs our planet. Hence they called their emperor the 'Son of Heaven', just as my ancestors in ancient India called our great rulers *Surya-vanshi* - descendants of the sun.

In 2073 BC when Chounn succeeded Yao, the first historical emperor of China, we can safely assume that he did not know the Second Law of Thermodynamics. According to this law, all organized systems degenerate towards disorganization. Why does the earth then continue to bloom with life? The reason is that the sun keeps infusing the planet with fresh energy. So, deduced the Chinese, must the rulers infuse their people with life.

Chounn therefore decided to begin his rule by offering a sacrifice to the 'Sovereign of the Sky', visiting the four sacred mountains located at the four points of the compass, and by surveying the propitious position of the

'Seven Rectors' (the sun, moon, and five planets). That decision was based on centuries of observation of the facts of the solar system. The observation itself was a legitimate 'science', although the interpretation of the observed facts was mistaken and its consequences for Chinese civilization disastrous. Later in this booklet we shall see some of the consequences of astrology in ancient civilizations: weakening the individual; lowering his/her value; and breeding superstitions, exploitation, fatalism and resignation in the face of all kinds of oppression.

In *Astrology in Roman Law and Politics*, Fr H. Cramer showed that periods of social upheaval are especially conducive to astrology - which could explain its present resurgence. Once Roman civilization entered its troubled period in 139 BC, almost every man and woman that mattered in the empire began to patronize astrologers. Emperor Tiberius used his court astrologer, Thrasyllus, to prepare the horoscopes of all the ambitious people at his court, so that he might execute those potential rivals whose stars seemed to favour the imperial throne! Yet, predictably, astrology could not save Rome, anymore than it could save the ancient Babylonian, Persian, Greek, Indian, or Chinese empires.

St Augustine - an incisive observer of the Roman world in the fifth century - observed that astrology was one of the factors that had weakened and destroyed Roman civilization. In his autobiographical classic *Confessions,* which dominated the intellectual scene in Europe for almost a thousand years, Augustine said that at one time he was seriously involved in studying astrology. He gave it up when he was persuaded that, a) an honest man could not earn a living by astrology since it was full of trickery and deceit; b) it robbed human beings of their dignity because it taught that they were not responsible for their own actions - their deeds were a result of the influence of Venus, or Mars, or Saturn; and c) when the predictions turned out to be true they were the result of chancc.

THE CENTRAL ISSUES

A discussion on astrology must however, answer questions such as: Why does astrology appear to work sometimes? Why have men and women in many generations and cultures intuitively felt that their destinies are bound up with their stars? Why do so many sincere and intelligent people today believe in astrology?

Even more basic questions needing to be answered are: What is a human being? What accounts for the dignity of the human race and for the uniqueness of each individual? Could it be the influence of the stars on us? Are we made in the image of our stars? Do the celestial bodies rule our destinies, or are they created to assist us in our task of ruling this earth?

THE ATTRACTION OF THE STARS

A woman would naturally believe an astrologer who claimed to be able to explain why her two previous marriages had fallen apart, why her present boyfriend was unwilling to make a lifelong commitment to her, and who would qualify as Mr Right, with whom she could have a stable, predictable relationship.

A culture that seriously believed that human beings were mere animals would naturally dehumanize people. It will use people, exploit them, treat them as animals, if not just as cogs in a machine, and then discard them. Every dehumanizing culture makes people insecure. It does not matter if the process of dehumanization takes place *illegally*, as in the case of rape, or *legally,* as in prostitution, polygamy, divorce or slavery. Dehumanization is disturbing. Astrology thrives in such troubled times for:

a. It offers an explanation for our troubles - 'our individual, national or global stars at this time are inauspicious'.

b. It removes a sense of guilt and responsibility from us - 'my marriage has fallen apart, not because of my selfishness, but because our stars were incompatible'.

c. It gives hope - 'our times will change for the better when the present configuration of the planets changes'.

d. It offers guidance when we are at our wits' ends - 'do (or do not) gamble on this option because your stars are favorable (or unfavorable)'.

Let us take up the practical issue related to astrology first and then return to these more basic questions.

WHAT MAKES ASTROLOGY WORK?

Three kinds of hypotheses regarding the influence of the stars appear worthy of consideration. The *first* is the belief that astrology is a science. Many believers in astrology hold this view, but not its serious proponents. This view assumes that there is a mechanical (or scientific cause-and-effect) relationship between ourselves and our zodiac sign. Therefore our stars influence, if not determine, all of our lives. This implies that astrology is a proper scientific study of horoscopes, although, runs the theory, it is often abused, or mixed with superstition.

An *alternative* modern hypothesis has become associated with the name of the great psychoanalyst Carl Jung, a disciple of Sigmund Freud. This theory postulates that astrological (and other) predictions come true neither by chance nor because stars cause them to happen in a physical sense. Some things are related to each other *meaningfully* though not *mechanically*. Jung called this phenomenon *synchronicity*. Others, following this general trend, propose that we are connected with our stars at some pre-atomic vibrational level, or that planets are in fact *sub-personalities* within ourselves, with lives of their own, and therefore they are able to influence us. There are several variations of this viewpoint today. Most of these views seek to combine astrology with physical or emotional therapy. The common thread running through these theories is that astrology is a real, but not a *mechanistic* science.

The *third* kind of hypothesis rejects the view that astrology has anything to do with stars and planets. Some authors such as Dan Korem, a Jewish magician-turned-psychic detective, argue that psychic and astrological readings are common-sense *cold-readings*. Other scholars, such

such as Dr Anthony Stone, a mathematics-professor, Sanskrit scholar, and authority on Hindu astrology, maintain that when there are genuine astrological predictions, their source is spiritualistic, not astrological. Let us examine some of these theories:

1. ASTROLOGY AS SCIENCE

Some years ago John H. Nelson, a scientist working for the Radio Corporation of America, was able to predict, with an astounding 93 per cent accuracy, the days on which radio reception would be poor. This was because he had found that good reception occurred when two or more planets were at the angles of 60 to 120 degrees relative to the sun, and bad reception occurred when the planets were at angles of 0, 90 to 180 degrees. He also found smaller effects at various multiples of 7.5 degrees.

Because 90 divided by 12 is 7.5, many intellectuals, including the prominent Indian scientist Dr B.V. Raman, have argued that Nelson's predictions are based on 'astrological data'.

Michel Gauquelin, a French scholar, makes many similar and significant observations in his book *The Cosmic Clocks*. For example, he points out that there is a shellfish that produces eggs only at full moons from January to July. Statistics in countries in the Northern Hemisphere show more than the average number of human births in May and June, and less than average in November and December. The sunspot cycle, of about eleven years on the average, coincides approximately with cycles in climate, plant and animal life, and even in economic and business trends. High tide occurs when the moon is in the fourth and tenth astrological houses, and low tide when the moon is in the first and seventh houses.

In recent decades, attempts have been made to study the horoscopes of top people in various professions to arrive at statistical conclusions about the reliability of horoscopes. Gauquelin's conclusion was that while professional success cannot always be correlated with specific planets, certain personality traits do correlate (at least statistically) with certain planets.

J.A. West and J.G. Toonder maintain in their book *The Case for Astrology* that the statistical results produced by correlating professional success with specific planets are crucial because the probability of obtaining these results by chance is only one in a million. Observations such as these lead many astrologers to conclude that the planets influence our lives directly, and therefore astrology is a legitimate science which studies and interprets planetary influences on human behavior.

We know that DNA inherited from our parents has an enormous influence on our physical and mental make-up. The DNA template stores information on what color our hair will be long before our skull even exists. There is a cause-and-effect relationship between DNA and our future development. Thus, it can be studied scientifically. Some simple-minded astrologers, anxious to establish their craft as a science, do argue that there is a similar cause-and-effect relationship between one's horoscope and one's life.

A horoscope is indeed a scientific, mathematical chart of the position of various heavenly bodies at the time of one's birth. An astronomer who rejects astrology as nonsense would cast exactly the same horoscope for us as an astrologer.

Two facts cannot be denied. First, that the influence of the celestial bodies is general, not specific. The moon's magnetic pull has to affect all the people in its path in a similar way, irrespective of their horoscopes. Secondly, different things react differently to the influence of the sun and the moon. Some creatures go to sleep with the sunset while others begin their work. Some flowers open with sunrise while others open with sunset. So the question is - even if a horoscope itself is a scientific chart from that 'natal chart', how does one arrive at a description of someone's personality, and at predictions about the future? How do we answer St Augustine's old objection about the twins? *Why do even identical twins, with the same genetic make up and the same horoscopes, turn out to be so different from each other?*

Some astrologers, such as India's mathematical genius Shakuntala Devi, affirm a belief in astrology because of the interconnectedness of everything in the universe. They refer to the discovery of the new physics, that electrons remain mysteriously 'interconnected' even when separated from each other. They assert that the interconnectedness of the electrons proves that we are also connected to heavenly bodies. The planets' movements, therefore, have a direct influence on us, just as the moon affects the tides of the oceans.

Everything in the universe is indeed interconnected. That is precisely what makes it impossible to single out a few stars and planets in the hope of understanding ourselves on the basis of their influence alone. Aren't we also connected to the underground minerals at the place of our birth? What about the influence of the building material of the hospital where we were born, and the trees near the place of our birth? How can we know ourselves and our future without knowing their influence?

Besides, if the interconnectedness of all things is to be taken seriously, then it has to be assumed that the planets also influence or determine our aeroplanes, trains, cars, taxis, houses, dogs, cows, and cats. Indeed, an increasing number of affluent Indians are now getting their trusted astrologers to make horoscopes for their dogs and their automobiles. Prominent Indian astrologers in New Delhi, who have given respectability to this trend include Pandit S.Nanjundaiah and Ms Geeta Sen. Could the people patronizing this new fad be bringing themselves into ever greater bondage and mental slavery, as in earlier ages of superstition?

Two kinds of objection to the claim that astrology is a science have never been satisfactorily answered. One concerns the nature of science, and the other the logical implications of a belief in astrological determinism.

(A) Astrology and the Nature of Science

We can often demonstrate that a medicine that heals a specific disease works in a scientific sense, i.e. it causes healing. Sometimes, however, a plain distilled-water injection can also cure a fever dramatically. So a magic stone, a mantra, a handful of 'holy ash', or a tablespoonful of honey and pepper can produce similar healing effects. It has, nevertheless, been shown that such healings are not 'caused' by the water or the holy ash. It is the patient's faith and expectation that triggers off the production of certain chemicals in the patient's brain which cause healing.

This should warn us that just because the movement of planets influences radio reception, we cannot naively deduce that everything in our life is impacted by them. Nor can we conclude, just because an astrologer correctly told a divorced woman that her teenage daughter is her biggest problem, that this proves that the stars determine our lives. We all know some 'wise old man' who can diagnose and predict things fairly accurately about us on the basis of their observation of human beings.

In the case of radio reception, it is 'planetary magnetic storms' that cause the changes. These storms are not fully understood as yet. But we know that to make his prediction, Nelson also had to consider factors other than planetary positions. These included the positions (relative to the sun) of the nodes of each planet, but his theories were later debunked.

Some serious astrologers recognize that the following factors make astrology an intuitive exercise in divination, not a scientific *discipline*.

The Planets

Astrologers get similar results by using different systems of astrology, each involving different sets of planets. Traditional Western astrology uses seven 'planets' - the sun, the moon, Mars, Jupiter, Mercury, Venus, and Saturn. Contemporary astrologers are struggling to incorporate planets such as Uranus, Neptune, and Pluto into their systems. The traditional Indian system uses nine planets. Seven of these are the same as in the Western system, the other two are the moon's nodes.

Different Indian and Western astrological systems also use some additional, unobserved, imaginary planets.

These can have no physical influence. On the other hand, in astrology most stars, planets, and asteroids are ignored. For that matter, the three-dimensional picture of the planetary and stellar position is generally ignored. Only the positions of arbitrarily chosen sets of planets are considered in the plane of the zodiacal sign; which means that astrology is not based on a scientific belief in the interconnectedness of all things. It has traditionally been rooted in the belief that the sun, moon, and planets are living beings - gods. The prevalence of such a belief amongst primitive people was understandable given the fact that these bodies were seen moving. The planets even seemed to stop for a while and 'wander' in the opposite direction before resuming their journey through the zodiac. But after the invention of telescopes it became difficult to believe that the planets were living beings.

If a distilled-water injection, a spoon of honey with pepper, a bitter herb, a magic stone, an aspirin, or an antibiotic all have the same healing effect, then the scientific inference would be that some other hidden factor is the real cause of healing. These 'medicines' only help that process begin. Likewise, if completely different systems work equally well, then we have to conclude that the planets play no intrinsic role in astrological prediction; some other factor is at work.

The Zodiac

The twelve signs of the zodiac, of 30 degrees each, were invented in Babylon in the fourth or fifth century BC. Each sign corresponds to a constellation, and was originally near that constellation. It was a brilliant scientific observation, which is extremely useful even today. The agreement about the zodiac was never exact, because stellations vary in size. The idea is still used in astronomy, because the twelve signs of the zodiac form an excellent reference system for the positions of the planets as seen from the earth. Astrology, however, mystifies the signs by ascribing various personal qualities to these impersonal - and in a sense even imaginary - entities.

Astrology does not treat the zodiacal signs any more scientifically than it does the planets. Western astrology, for example, uses what are called tropical signs, beginning with the sun's position at the beginning of spring. Indian astrological systems, on the other hand, work with sidereal signs starting with various fixed points among the stars. (Sidereal simply means 'fixed star').

Another unscientific aspect of astrology is the arbitrary way in which the zodiac is divided into twelve parts relative to the horizon. Some experts believe that originally only eight so-called 'houses' were used. Some astrological systems now use ten houses, others twenty-four and some even forty-eight houses.

It is possible, but not necessary, to study other factors that contradict astrology's claim to be a science. For example, the method of timing future events. Western astrology uses at least five different methods, Indian astrology forty-five. Genuine science is continually correcting itself by rejecting inadequate theories or methods. Astrology retains all methods because it is an authoritarian system, where rules are not usually explained, examined, or defended.

In science, there is a real and direct connection between a cause and its effect. Therefore it is repeatable (except when relevant factors are beyond human control), and can realistically strive for 100 per cent success. Astrology uses only a symbolic connection between planets and human beings. Thus it makes free use of chance and intuition and only hopes for success.

Science progresses because it keeps rejecting disproved theories and is quick to accept a theory as soon as its validity has been substantiated. What is static is generally a pseudo-science. Rolf M. Sinclair made this point with reference to Astrology in 1980, in San Francisco, at a meeting of the American Association for the Advancement of Science. He pointed out that, 'Astrology froze about two thousand years ago and simply hasn't changed much. That unchanging character is what allows me to say that astrology is a pseudo-science.'

The dramatic growth of astrology today symbolizes the fact that although technology is advancing, the scientific spirit is dying before our eyes, and people are increasingly anxious. Science arose in a Christian intellectual milieu that insisted on finding out objective truth. During the sixteenth century, Reformation Protestantism, or rather, biblical Christianity challenged traditional beliefs with questions such as: 'Is this really so?' The Bible assumed that the human mind was able to know true truth about the universe because (a) our rationality was made in the image of God who had made the cosmos with his infinite reason and, (b) rationality was given to us precisely so that we may understand nature and establish our rule over it.

The twentieth-century idea that the universe is a product of blind chance and not an intelligent design undermined our confidence in human rationality. How can reason understand that which is an irrational product of chance? Modern 'chance painting' and 'chance music' demonstrated that products of blind chance cannot be deciphered rationally. As confidence in our rationality and in objective truth is now declining, the important consideration today is not, 'Is this really so?' but, 'Does it feel good to you?' Astrology grows not because it is true, but because it feels good to have an authoritative guide in a mindless universe.

(B) Implications of Astrological Determinism

The belief that astrology is a science means that it is a study of the causal, predictable effects of the movements and positions of the celestial entities on our personality, work, achievements, and relationships. If the heavenly bodies are impersonal entities, then there is little we can do to change their influence. Each of us is a pawn in their 'hands'. Astrology then robs us of our dignity - we are not responsible for our actions; we cannot hope to set our own goals and work towards achieving them; we can neither take satisfaction in our achievements nor hold anyone accountable for their failures.

We can only hope to talk to the planets, appease them, and make them change their minds if they are persons - gods or spirits. But that would make astrology a religion and not a science. It would be a bad religion for the simple reason that it makes our gods venal - gods that use their powers to harass us and extract bribes from us.

Astrology must also undermine science. If the future prospects of a child depend upon his or her being born at an auspicious time, then it is better to have the astrologer, and not the doctor, decide the moment of the Caesarean section. In India, many couples already put the astrologer above the doctor.

The sun, of course, does not make a rose red or yellow. It is the genetic make-up of a rose that determines which shade of the spectrum it will absorb and which it will reflect. The factors that make each person unique are primarily internal - our heredity, our learning, our beliefs, and choices. If planets in fact determined our personality traits, then identical twins could not be so different.

2. A NON-SCIENTIFIC LINK BETWEEN THE STARS AND OURSELVES?

Does every effect have to have a physical and knowable cause? A fundamental presupposition of modern science has been that the 'law of causation' is an absolute and inviolable principle. However, there are effects which have no knowable cause - yet. For example, both theoretically as well as experimentally, radioactive decay is totally unpredictable. It is an effect with no knowable cause. Facts such as this have now raised fundamental doubts about whether physical causation is adequate as a full explanation of reality.

Consequently many thinkers have begun to put forward alternative theories such as *seriality* and *synchronicity* to explain how astrology could be true without the stars actually causing or determining events in our lives. In 1919, Paul Kammerer, a Viennese experimental biologist, propounded his *law of seriality*. For twenty years, Kammerer had maintained a log-book of coincidences in his life. His book, *Das Gesetz der Serie*, contains one hundred selected coincidences. On the basis of these, he defines seriality as the concurrence in space or the recurrence in time of meaningfully, but not causally, connected events.

Synchronicity was the idea developed by the Nobel laureate physicist Wolfgang Pauli and the psychoanalyst Carl Jung, whose essay, 'Synchronicity: An Acausal Connecting Principle', published in 1952, widely popularized the concept and made it a possible justification for belief in paranormal events such as telepathy, clairvoyance, and divination, including astrology.

However, the notions of seriality and synchronicity are so vague that they do not explain anything. The main contribution of the ideas is that they weaken a purely rationalistic and mechanistic view of reality. There are other writers who attempt explanations of unexplained phenomena as 'the vibrations of the cosmos on the earth'. If the essence of the planets and of our own selves is some spiritual vibration, then it is not all that far-fetched to assume that the planets implant our personalities in us. Therefore, many people today use astrology more for psychotherapy than for physical therapy.

According to this school of thought, some of our sub-personalities actually correspond to our planets. The objective of studying astrology is therefore to become increasingly aware of all the personalities within us, so that we do not allow just one or two of these planets to run our lives, but make decisions in consultation with all of the personalities within us.

This understanding of astrology sounds new because it is presented in contemporary psychological language. However, many ancient cultures have thought of heavenly bodies as spirits - *stoicheia* in Greek. The English versions of the New Testament often translate *stoicheia* as 'spirits' or 'principles' (e.g., Galatians 4:3,9 and Colossians 2:8, 20). But as Dr Wim Rietkerk says in his book *The Future Great Planet Earth*, 'These "spirits" (and "principles") sometimes were identified with stars and configurations of stars in the same way as astrologers do today.' Whether our connection with the planets is understood as vibrational or in terms of sub-personalities, the point is that this viewpoint is honest in admitting astrology is outside the limits of physical science and rational discussion. Some of them also admit that astrology is not a science but an aspect of spiritualism.

3. ASTROLOGICAL OR SPIRITUALISTIC GUIDANCE?

If astrology is not a science, then how do some astrologers get good results? The mathematician-turned-Sanskrit scholar Dr Anthony Stone's extensive studies in Hindu astrology led him to the conclusion that when astrologers do get accurate results, which cannot be attributed to chance or common sense, then their predictions are often communications received from spirits or demons.

A prediction that appeals to our common sense could still be harmful. For example, an astrologer obviously gets the attention of a man when he begins his interpretation of his horoscope with a correct statement that his biggest problem is his wife or his teenage son . He may explain the phenomenon with a claim that this is so because the man is an 'earth sign' whereas the wife or the son is an incompatible 'water sign'! This 'insight' might amaze the man and he may fail to see that all our closest relationships do give us the greatest pain, in an age when virtues such as obedience and self-sacrifice are devalued and a premium is put on individual self-fulfilment. Yet, these relationships are also our greatest riches. Should a single mother look upon her rebellious child as her problem or as her greatest asset, with a challenge to build a relationship of love, respect, and obedience?

Let us, for a moment, accept the possibility that some astrologers make accurate predictions because they happen to be in touch with the *stoicheia* or the spirits of astrology. What are the consequences of such knowledge?

To begin with, we have no way of knowing how much to trust these spirits. Every con man deceives us after winning our confidence by saying the right things. If human beings lie and deceive after winning our trust, how do we know that the disembodied spirits will not? A bigger problem, of course, is that such a spiritualistic knowledge undermines our responsibility to live by our rationality and to be accountable for our choices. Are we to govern our own lives under God? Or, are we allowed to hand over the responsibility of making crucial decisions for our lives to some spirit whom we cannot hold accountable?

People consult their astrologers when they are confronted with crucial choices in life. What if their errors were to decide the major turning points of your life? Do we not violate our own dignity when we decide not to make the important decisions of our life ourselves? Can we stand before God at the end of our life and say, 'I should not be blamed for ruining my life and opportunities because I had handed over the responsibility for my life to someone I didn't even know?' What if God responded, 'That was your biggest mistake? Your life was given to you; why then did you hand over your decision-making to another? Why did you choose to live your life on the basis of fear and slavery, instead of living by faith as my child?' We need to look more carefully at:

DANGERS OF DEFINING OURSELVES IN TERMS OF OUR STARS

When we say, 'I am angry because I have a difficult Mars,' or, 'I need freedom and variety in love relationships because I have Venus square Uranus', we do have a kind of knowledge of ourselves. But this method of discovering and defining ourselves has several inherent dangers that are a result of the fact that the planets are impersonal whereas we are personal.

The first danger in defining ourselves in terms of the stars is that we begin to fit the dynamic complexity of human personality into a neat little box. What should I do if, because of my stars, I have a problem with anger and inability to forgive? If I change, am I struggling against my creators? Astrological self- knowledge tends to become bondage rather than liberating truth.

King Solomon, famous for his legendary wisdom, observed: 'A gentle answer turns away wrath, but a harsh word stirs up anger' (Proverbs 15:1). St Paul exhorts us: 'Do not let the sun go down while you are still angry, and do not give the devil a foothold' (Ephesians 4:26-7). When my father, an extremely patient man, had a disagreement with my mother, he would not talk to her for days. I inherited this trait. I have had to assume that I inherited it from him and not from my planets, because we were born under different signs. The problem could have destroyed my marriage on several occasions. As St Paul put it, my bottled-up hurt and anger (or sulking) really 'gives the devil a foothold.' Suppose I believe that I sulk because that is what my stars have made me? Should I conform to my creators or struggle against them? I need to change. I need grace to apologise and strength to forgive. I have no natural inner power to obey the injunction to 'let the sun not go down on [my] anger'. I need outside help.

Obviously, I am a sinner. But if this trait in me is the influence of my stars, then there is little I can do about it. My perspective, however, would be different if the truth is that human beings were made in the image of a perfect God and later became sinful. In that case my need is not to know my stars but my Creator. Perhaps he might even re-form his image in me if I humble myself before him and ask for his grace and forgiveness. The fact is that had my marriage been dependent on our horoscopes, it would have ended a long time ago. My wife and I are opposite and incompatible. Our marriage survives because when I hate, God's command rings louder, 'Husbands love your wives.' I have learned that for their survival, marriages need not the matching of horoscopes but obedience to God's command; a desire to be like God who loves us even when we are rebellious.

Before I submitted myself to God I had no control over my tongue. Through prayer I have now learnt to bring another's anger to an end with a soft answer. This inner transformation is based on the philosophical underpinning that I am made not in the image of impersonal stars, but a personal God. Like all other human beings I too am a sinner. But I can be saved and transformed to become more like my heavenly Father. The astrological chart, at best, only tells us what we are. God tells us both what we are and what we ought be and how to become like him.

The astrological approach to self -knowledge turns us into objects: Mars, or Venus, or Saturn has done this, that, or the other to me. Human beings, however, are subjects, not objects. Self-consciousness is our essence. It enables us to say, 'I am this, that, or the other, but I can change'.

A second danger in seeking self-knowledge through astrology results from the fact that astrology uses highly abstract symbols. The more we attempt to fit ourselves into abstract categories, the less we will be able to know ourselves as we truly are. A better way of discovering ourselves is through in-depth, lasting relationships with real people and by reading biographies.

I have found that reading the Bible every day is a very effective way of getting to know myself. This is because the Bible contains literally hundreds of realistic biographies from many different cultures, covering a very long historical period. We can know ourselves better by knowing real people. Abstract symbols can be helpful but our generation, more than previous generations, is in need of real heroes and models. This is because most of us have known only celluloid heroes and models from the unreal world of high-tech advertising. Discovering ourselves from our horoscopes can be comforting or paralysing, but discovering ourselves by looking at real heroes is always challenging and uplifting. Most importantly, I love reading the Bible because it helps me know God. He alone knows our present, past and future, our conscious as well as our unconscious self. We need to see ourselves as he sees us. That is indispensable if we want to become what he wants us to be.

A third danger in seeking to know ourselves astrologically is that we reduce ourselves to concepts. People can be categorized into personality types, such as sanguine, choleric, phlegmatic, and melancholic, but our self-concepts never equal our real self. We are far more complex than any intellectual description or psychological analysis of ourselves. Therefore, experience and intuition are more profound means of personal knowledge than self-concepts. Knowing ourselves implies taking responsibility for ourselves. It includes repenting of what we have been; setting higher goals for ourselves irrespective of what our horoscope says. It involves growing in faith, hope and love.

Our self-concepts are not realities, but they can influence us. If I read Christ's parable of the Good Samaritan in the morning, I might decide to try and be a good neighbor to the people I meet. At the end of the day, I would have made new friends and deepened existing relationships. But if I read my horoscope and find that I am likely to be rejected today, I will assume an aloof and defensive posture. My expectation and manner will make that astrological prediction a self-fulfilling prophecy - I will be rejected.

ASTROLOGY AND RELATIONSHIPS

Most marriages among Hindus are arranged only after an astrologer has established that the horoscopes of the boy and the girl match. As faith in astrology has grown in the West, people are increasingly prejudging others on the basis of their horoscopes. It distorts their attitude to other people. To pigeonhole our complex dynamic personalities is bad enough; to prejudge others is certainly worse. It could be more destructive of relationships than allowing first impressions to be the last impressions.

If your colleague, spouse or child is *expecting* you to be cross or angry, he or she is likely to misinterpret your words or acts. Instead of judging your action or reaction at its face value, they will judge it in the light of their preconceived idea of how you may be feeling. When we habitually prejudge people astrologically, these kinds of misconceptions and misconstructions are bound to happen more often and harm relationships. Strong relationships are built on love, trust and respect for the other person. They involve forgiving those who hurt us and finding inner strength to bring the best out of others

A relationship is worthwhile when it is based on mutual give and take, when each partner makes sacrifices for the other and adjusts to their needs and wishes. The problem with the planets is that our relationship with them is only one way. They influence us but we cannot change them.

ASTROLOGICAL POWER: CAN KNOWLEDGE WEAKEN AND ENSLAVE?

It is frightening to be alone in an impersonal universe and a selfish society where people we love and trust the most could end up hurting us the most. When we stand at important crossroads, the fear of an unknown future could be paralysing, especially if we feel that we do not have the resources to cope. Astrologers can be a source of power in these settings, especially if they make positive, comforting predictions.

Paradoxically, however, the very knowledge of the future can be a weakening experience in a deeper way. When we are watching a thriller movie, knowing the end lessens the fear and tension of the moment, but our enjoyment is not as great as when we go through the thrill without knowing what is at the end of the tunnel.

King David, who went through many hopelessly dark tunnels in his life, said: 'Even though I walk through the valley of the shadow of death, I will fear no evil, for you are with me; your rod and your staff, they comfort me. You prepare a table before me in the presence of my enemies' (Psalm 23: 4-5).

David found strength, not by knowing what the future held for him, but by knowing the One who holds up the stars. Indeed, the stronger men and women are those who persevere in faith, hope, and love in the midst of suffering and hardships without knowing when, if ever, these will end. Who is better placed to face the evils that come our way: a person who knows that his future is planned by a heavenly Father, or a person who believes that a capricious planet like Saturn is in charge of his life at this time?

St Paul faced violent persecution, financial difficulties and horrendous natural disasters such as shipwrecks in stormy seas. Yet he said, 'We know that in all things God works for the good of those who love Him' (Romans 8:28).

St Paul was only one of the many prophets, saints and mahatmas who strongly opposed astrology.

INDIAN AND HEBREW OPPOSITION TO ASTROLOGY

Mahatma Jotiba Phule, the first 'low-caste' social reformer in India, in the middle of the nineteenth century, attacked astrology in his influential book of ballads, *Priest-craft Exposed*. Like St Augustine, he saw that (while some astrologers might be sincere individuals) astrology had become a means of deceitful exploitation of the innocent masses by unscrupulous priests.

Phule showed how astrology in India was the chief means of priestly deceit and exploitation from a person's birth until his death. It was Mahatma Phule's study of the Bible which convinced him that an important task of the Indian social reformer had to be to liberate people from astrology. Since astrology had made Indians superstitious, fatalistic and vulnerable to exploitation, it had turned our priests into crooks and our gods into oppressive and corrupt beings. Mahtma Phule's encounter with the British helped him realize that nineteenth-century Western civilization was only the second civilization in history to be freed from the fatalism that follows fortune-telling. Hebrew civilization was the first, because the Bible banned all forms of divination, including astrology.

Many Indian thinkers have followed Phule in this attempt to free us from superstitions, exploitation and fatalism. Nirad Chaudhuri was one of India's greatest writers in the twentieth century. In his *Autobiography of an Unknown Indian* he pointed out that one reason for India's corruption is that our gods and goddesses are venal, i.e., they demand to be appeased and take bribes.

Our astrological deities routinely use their power

to harass people until appeased with bribes. So every Indian ruler and officer becomes godly, that is god-like. He uses his power to create difficulties for people and extort bribes. It is because of this religious worldview, wrote Nirad Chaudhuri, that the atmosphere in an Indian police station has become like the atmosphere in a Hindu temple, and 'morality (has) received its worst blow from what is popularly believed to be its patron and protector.'

One of Mahatma Phule's inspirations was Moses, the greatest leader and prophet of the Jews. Moses grew up in the palace of the Egyptian Pharaoh and studied all existing Egyptian knowledge. He did not reject Egyptian astronomy. He knew that the sun and moon govern our planet and that they must be studied because they were 'signs'. But what are they signs of? They help us divide the universe of vast space and time into understandable, and therefore manageable, parts. Maps, clocks and calendars - our basic tools for planning and organizing life - are made possible because of these heavenly bodies. How do we know what is East or West? How can sailors chart routes across oceans? How do we divide time into days, months and years?

Moses, who wrote most of the first five books of the Bible, explained that these celestial entities were not gods. They were objects created by God. They must be studied because God had created them for specific beneficial purposes. God did make the sun, moon and other heavenly bodies to govern the earth - its motion, seasons and eco-systems. The sun does tell creatures when to sleep and when to wake up. But God created human beings as his children to rule over this earth. We are to use the heavenly bodies as our assistants to establish our culture or 'dominion' on the earth. The sun may say it is time to sleep or to wear woolen clothing, but we have the authority to say 'No thank you! We still have work to do. So we will decide when it will be dark in our home, workplace or sportsfield. And we will determine what the temperature will be in our home, class or car.' To allow the sun to rule our lives is to become a slave. As God's image-bearers , we are created to rule.

Mahatma Phule's mission was to liberate the 'untouchables' in India from their slavery to Brahminism. He was inspired by Moses whose mission had been to liberate the Hebrews from their slavery in Egypt. Moses knew that his people's political slavery in Egypt was a minor, external matter. Astrology and other forms of divination and fortune telling were far more destructive of our humanness than political slavery. Fortune-telling made people internalize their slavery. What would be gained if the Hebrews were freed from the slavery of Egyptians only to be enslaved by cunning fellow Hebrews in a permanent and radical way? Fatalism would permanently paralyse their culture. So Moses was not horrified when God commanded capital punishment for Hebrews who indulged in astrology, spiritualism and other forms of divination. God was liberating the Hebrews from their slavery. He was not going to permit them to enslave each other in such a radical way that they were permanently dehumanized. As his children, they were to be rulers over nature, not ruled by inanimate nature by proxy of crafty priests.

Let us now return to a more basic issue raised by astrology.

WHAT IS MAN? AND WHAT MAKES HUMAN BEINGS UNIQUE?

We are a part of nature and dependent on nature. But we are unique in that we also impose the fruit of our imagination on nature, thereby creating culture. What God creates is nature; what we create is culture. The greatness of a given culture is substantially dependent upon its ability to bring more and more of nature under responsible human management. A tribe that fears, worships, or flows with nature does not create a great culture. Culture involves not merely understanding and harnessing oxen and horses; wind, water or steam; electricity, fossil oils or atomic energy, but also sun, moon, solar system, and galaxies.

Today we can place satellites in the sky and see the whole globe simultaneously in one room. We can understand and predict global weather, and so plan and manage life on this planet more efficiently. Why? This became possible because the Bible freed Western civilization from astrology and other forms of fatalism that dehumanize us. They breed fear of nature and the future, paralysing us, and sapping our creative powers.

The biblical understanding of time and our relation to it is one of the most important foundations of the remarkable development of Western civilization which created the modern world. In astrologically-determined cultures such as India, we did not plan and manage our time. We believed that we do not rule over time, but that our times rule our destiny. Traditionally, it was not our corporation's business plan but our horoscopes that decided when we would travel, or do deals.

Thus, the choice for or against faith in astrology

becomes a choice between looking at ourselves as above time or under it: of governing time or being governed by it.

RECOVERING HUMAN DIGNITY

For those who give astrology an important place in their lives, it increasingly becomes a source of weakness, fearfulness and dependency. That happens because they experience themselves as victims; footballs that are kicked around by forces more powerful than themselves; people who are acted upon, rather than individuals who are created to go out and subdue the earth and govern their environment. Therefore, it should not come as a surprise to us that God asks his children not to indulge in divination or to fear astrological signs:

> Do not learn the ways of the nations or be terrified by signs in the sky, though the nations are terrified by them. For the customs of the peoples are worthless . . . (Jeremiah 10:2-3).

The New Testament says the following to those who once knew themselves by knowing God, but later began to seek knowledge, power and reality through their stars:

> When we were children, we were in slavery under the basic principles [*stoicheia* - the stars or spirits] . . . But now that you know God - or rather are known by God- how is it that you are turning back to those weak and miserable principles [*stoicheia*]? Do you wish to be enslaved by them all over again? You are observing special days and months and seasons and years! I fear for you, that somehow I have wasted my efforts on you (Galatians 4:3, 9-11).

St Paul wrote to those who loved God in the Greek city of Colosse that he was struggling for them, so that they

> may have the full riches of complete understanding, in order that they may know the mystery of God, namely, Christ, in whom are hidden all the treasures of wisdom and knowledge. I tell you this so that no one may deceive you by fine-sounding arguments . . . See to it that no one takes you captive through hollow and deceptive philosophy, which depends on human tradition and the basic principles of this world [i.e., *the stoicheia,* or spirits of astrology] rather than on Christ (Colossians 2:2-4, 8).

To summarize, the most important question for anyone thinking about astrology is whether we are made in the image of our stars or in the image of the God who made the stars and rules over them. Our answer to that question will determine whether, in a given culture, human beings will manage and rule over time, or whether time will rule over them. To put it differently, the issue is whether the stars are created to govern us or to assist us in our task of governing the planet.

FINDING MEANING AND GUIDANCE FOR DAILY LIFE

A deeper philosophical problem with astrology is that it cannot provide a meaning to our lives because the stars are a finite reference point. They leave us without any ultimate meaning because we have to find an infinite reference point to find real - in contrast to merely existential - meaning. Jean Paul Sartre, the French existential philosopher, put it this way: 'No finite point can have any meaning unless it has an infinite reference point.'

My studies in philosophy taught me that I can find ultimate meaning for my life only in my relationship with the infinite, personal God. I am a unique, self-conscious, rational, creative, moral person because I am made in his image. I cannot talk to the stars because they are not persons. God, however, is a Person who can and does love me. Therefore, he is someone I can talk to and expect to respect my personhood and my personal needs. Because God is infinite, I can expect him not only to guide me into the unknown future but also to change my personal, social and natural circumstances, according to my needs and his plans for my good.

As a teenager I knew that I was a sinner because I deliberately made evil choices. I could not blame my stars because my conscience confirmed what the Bible told me, that (a) I was responsible for my sin, and (b) that it was my sin which separated me from my family, friends, and God. The Bible told me that God does not use his power to harass innocent people and demand gifts from them. Rather God in the person of Jesus Christ sacrificed himself on the cross for the forgiveness of my sin. I found forgiveness and reconciliation with God through repentance for sin, and reconciliation with God through repentance for sin, and faith in Christ's self-sacrifice for my sin. Since I have become God's child, I have found that I can pray to my loving and almighty Father and find his guidance in the difficult situations of life. I have found that God not only guides me, but that he also provides for my physical, emotional, and social needs:

Day by day and with each passing moment

Strength I find to meet my trials here.

Trusting in my Father's wise bestowment

I've no cause for worry or for fear.

He whose heart is kind beyond all measure,

Gives unto each day what He deems best,

Lovingly its part of pain and pleasure

Mingling toil with peace and rest.

(Carolina V. Sandell Berg, 1865; translation by A. L. Skoog)

Jesus answered,

"I am the way and the truth and the life. ... and I will ask the Father, and he will give you another Counselor to be with you forever - the Spirit of truth. ... When he, the Spirit of truth, comes, he will guide you into all truth."

(John 14:6, 16-17; 16:13)

References

Ankerberg, J., and Weldon, J. *Astrology: Do the Heavens Rule Our Destiny?* (Eugene, OR: Harvest House, 1989).

Chaudhuri, Nirad, *Autobiography of an Unknown Indian* (Bombay : Jaico Publishing House, 1964)

Cramer, Fr H., *Astrology in Roman Law and Politics* from Memoirs of the American Philosophical Society, 37 (Philadelphia: American Philosophical Society, 1954).

Korem, D., *Powers: Testing The Psychic & Supernatural* (Downers Grove, IL: InterVarsity Press, 1988).

Gauquelin, Michel, *The Cosmic Clock* (London: Granada, 1980).

Phule, Mahatma Jotiba, Priest-craft Exposed from *Collected Works of Mahatma Jotirao Phule*, Vol.II (Bombay : Education Dept., Govt. of Maharashtra,1991).

Rietkerk, Dr Wim, *The Future Great Planet Earth (Good Books*, Mussoorie, India: Nivedit Good Books Distributors, 1989).

Stone, Dr Anthony, *Hindu Astrology* (New Delhi: Select Books, 1981).

West, J.A and Toonder, J.G., *The Case for Astrology* (Harmondsworth: Penguin Books, 1973)

Notes

Notes

Notes

Notes

Notes

OTHER BOOKLETS IN THE *WISDOM FROM INDIA* SERIES

1. Astrology

2. Yoga

3. Vegetarianism

4. Reincarnation

5. Mysticism

6. Suffering

7. Idolatry

8. Tolerance

9. New Physics and Metaphysics

10. The True Guru

See Last Page for Ordering.

OTHER BOOKS BY VISHAL MANGALWADI

1. The World of Gurus

2. In Search of Self: Beyond the New Age

3. Truth and Social Reform

4. India: The Grand Experiment

5. Missionary Conspiracy

6. What Liberates A Woman? The Story of Pandita Ramabai (with Nicol McNicol)

7. Corruption Vs. True Spirituality (with Francis A. Schaeffer)

8. Burnt Alive (with Vijay Martis and others)

See Last Page for Ordering.

To order the ***Wisdom from India*** booklets and/or other titles by Vishal Mangalwadi contact :

USA

South Asian Resources
Post Box 453, Willernie, MN 55090-0453
< SAResources@hotmail.com>

Canada

South Asian Resources
PO Box 51006
Unit 111-25 Peel Centre Drive,
Brampton, ON L6T 5M2
< SARCanada@yahoo.com>

Europe

Pippa Rann Books
Im Motteli 9, Magdenaustrasse,
CH-8570 Weinfelden, Switzerland.
<prb@europe.com>

UK

South Asian Concern
PO Box 43, Surrey, SM2 5WL, UK.
<100126.3641@compuserve.com>

Asia

Nivedit Good Books Distributors Pvt. Ltd.
Ivy Cottage, Landour, Mussoorie (Uttaranchal),
248 179 INDIA
<ruth@giasdlo1.vsnl.net.in>